D1126539

Recycling
Resources

Laurence Pringle

Recycling Resources

MACMILLAN PUBLISHING CO., INC.
New York
COLLIER MACMILLAN PUBLISHERS
London

The author wishes to thank Mr. John Ruf, Chief, Solid Waste
Management Branch, Region II, United States Environmental
Protection Agency, for reading and suggesting changes in the
manuscript of this book.

LIBRARY OF CONGRESS CATALOGING IN PUBLICATION DATA

Pringle, Laurence P   Recycling resources.

Bibliography: p.
1. Recycling (Waste, etc.)—Juvenile literature.
[1. Recycling (Waste)] I. Title.
TD794.5.P74   301.31   72–81062   ISBN 0–02–775310–7

contents

1   Down in the Dumps   *1*

2   Return or Throw Away?   *17*

3   Rescuing Resources   *31*

4   Paper and Plastics   *53*

5   Cars, Cans, Cloth, and Glass   *69*

6   Design for Recycling   *91*

What You Can Do   *109*

Further Reading   *113*

Index   *115*

Recycling
Resources

chapter 1
down in the dumps

Take a really different kind of hike some day. Go walking in a dump. There are thousands of dumps near towns and cities in North America. At a dump you will see some amazing and exciting things, and some disgusting and depressing things. You will get a close-up view of a problem that is sometimes called the "Third Pollution"—what to do with solid wastes.

Solid wastes are the things you toss into wastebaskets and other trash containers every day. They are the things you put into cans, boxes, or plastic bags and take to the curb for the "garbage men" to take away. You hear the garbage truck rumble up, the sound of the wastes being dumped aboard, empty trash cans rattling and crashing. Then the truck moves down the street. Your garbage, junk, refuse, trash—whatever you want to call it—is gone. Out of sight, out of mind.

A visit to a dump brings it back to mind. Somewhere you may have read that each person in the United States throws away six pounds of trash each day. At a dump it is plain to see that everyone is really doing it. The evidence is spread before you—acre after acre of cans, newspapers, plastic wrappers, broken toys, magazines, bottles, chunks of wood, light bulbs, broken television sets, lawn clippings, smashed grocery carts, chicken bones, paper plates, orange rinds, empty paint buckets, automobile tires.

Truck after truck brings fresh supplies of wastes from homes, stores, schools, restaurants, and hospitals. Hundreds of gulls circle overhead, waiting to settle down for a feast. The place is rich with sights, sounds, and smells.

The problems of solid waste disposal have not been in the news as much as the problems of air and water pollution. However, some experts consider this "Third Pollu-

Hundreds of gulls feast on garbage at dumps and

tion" to be a more serious environmental threat because so little is being done to solve it.

Getting rid of trash has been a problem ever since some early human first tossed a broken bone out the cave entrance. In fact, one way we learn about early humans is by studying their trash. Ancient garbage dumps are called kitchen middens by archaeologists. By studying the bones, broken pots, and tools that make up most of the contents of kitchen middens, archaeologists can discover a great deal about how people lived long ago. Today our trash heaps reveal much about our wasteful ways of living.

Early humans got rid of trash by burning, burying, or

landfills near the Great Lakes and ocean coasts.

putting it somewhere out of the way. The same methods are used today. Unlike early humans, however, we cannot simply pack up and move when the garbage heap gets too big and smelly. If that were a practical solution today, people living in many cities in the United States would soon have to move elsewhere. During the 1970s, nearly half of all cities may run out of places to put solid wastes.

More than 250 million tons of trash are collected each year by cities and towns in the United States. Trash collection and disposal costs $5 billion a year. In most cities, only schools and welfare cost more.

More than 14,000 towns and cities still put their wastes in open dumps. This is the cheapest method of waste disposal. But dumps stink. They are ideal living places for such disease-carrying animals as rats and houseflies. They pollute streams and underground water supplies. Dumps are sometimes set afire in order to reduce the volume of wastes. Whether deliberate or accidental, dump fires pollute the air. Wind scatters paper and other lightweight trash, spreading the dump's ugliness. No one likes to live or work near a dump, so nearby homes and land lose value. Dumps are cheap only in terms of the cost per ton of trash disposal. They are quite costly when all of their bad environmental effects are added up.

Some cities and towns put wastes in sanitary landfills. The word "sanitary" means clean, healthy, free of disease. No landfill is sanitary, though landfills are cleaner and neater than dumps. Like dumps, landfills are built in low-lying areas. Each day the wastes are spread in a layer and covered with about six inches of soil. Heavy bulldozers roll over the earth, packing down the trash and soil. Other lay-

4

Soil is spread and packed down over layers of solid wastes.

ers of wastes and earth are added on top. A properly maintained landfill smells better than a dump and does not burn.

Some landfill "mountains" have been built, but usually the filling stops when it reaches the level of the surrounding countryside. Then a last layer of soil, usually two feet deep, is spread over the wastes. Underground the garbage, paper, and other organic (once-living) materials gradually decay. This causes the landfill to settle, a process that goes on for at least five years. Although landfills are not safe places on which to place buildings, they can be used as parking lots, playgrounds, and golf courses. Land-

5

fills have been described as "a massive sweeping of dirt under a bright green rug."

Just because a sign saying "sanitary landfill" hangs at the entrance to a waste disposal site, that does not mean it is really a landfill. A survey in 1968 showed that only 6 percent of all disposal sites in the United States were genuine landfills. City officials prefer the name "sanitary landfill" to "dump." One state passed a law forbidding dumps. The law is poorly enforced, however, and most communities simply changed the names of their dumps to landfills. In other states, some genuine landfills are called dumps; this adds to the public confusion over the two names.

Landfills may be used for recreation areas and parks, such as this one in New Jersey.

About 90 percent of the solid waste collected in communities is put in landfills and dumps. The rest is burned in incinerators. There are about 300 large and 200 small city incinerators in the United States, plus thousands of even smaller ones in apartment houses, hospitals, schools, shopping centers, and industrial plants. Unfortunately, most of them were built before laws were passed to protect the quality of the air. Many incinerators lack even the most simple air pollution controls. Because of this, many have been shut down. Others may eventually have to close because cities cannot afford the expense of installing modern air pollution control equipment. The few modern incinerators now working produce little air pollution.

Incinerators do not burn metals, glass, and some other materials, but they do reduce the volume of trash by as much as 90 percent. Incinerator residues, or leftovers, are usually put in landfills, where they take up much less space than unburned refuse does.

Even with the help of incinerators, landfill space is rapidly being used up. Many cities cannot find new landfill sites. In the past they sometimes used swamps, marshes, river banks, and even parts of parks. Now the value of these natural areas is better known. They are no longer considered "wasteland," and people fight to keep them from being buried under tons of trash.

People also fight to keep dumps, landfills, and incinerators away from their homes. As one city official said, "Everyone wants us to pick up their garbage, but no one wants us to put it down."

Land is expensive too, and if cities are lucky enough to find a new landfill site, they have to pay a lot for it. Usually

about 20 percent of the cost of managing solid wastes lies in buying and maintaining disposal sites. The remaining 80 percent comes from collecting wastes and bringing them to the disposal sites. As cities use up nearby landfills and have to use more distant disposal sites, the cost of transporting trash will rise.

In city after city, officials have discovered that they face a solid waste crisis. The wastes keep coming, and soon there will be no place to put them.

One area with this problem is in northeastern New Jersey, close to New York City. Most of a 20,000-acre area called the Hackensack Meadowlands is being covered with landfill. The Hackensack Meadowlands Development Commission is required by law to dispose of the solid wastes from 118 New Jersey communities. All together these communities produce almost half of the state's solid wastes. But by the end of 1975 there will be no more landfill space in the Meadowlands.

Realizing this, in 1971 the commission announced a plan to build an incinerator. The incinerator would take in 6,000 tons of waste daily.

Many people objected to the plan. First, there wasn't enough time in which to build the incinerator before land-fill space ran out. Even if the incinerator reduced the volume of wastes by 90 percent, there would be 600 tons of residues to dispose of each day. Also, the amount of waste from the 118 communities is increasing each year. In just a few years—by 1980—the incinerator would be able to take in only half of the expected wastes. Finally, even with

The Hackensack Meadowlands has served as New Jersey's wastebasket.

9

air pollution control devices, the incinerator would send a thousand tons of soot into the air each year.

Faced with these objections, the commission turned to other solutions, including the idea of hauling wastes by train to distant landfills, perhaps in another state. Another plan would involve building four "reclamation" plants that would each take in 2,000 tons of solid wastes daily. The goals of this plan are to stop wasting valuable materials in trash and to bury as little as possible. The refuse would be shredded and metals and glass sorted out. Some

of the wastes might be used as fuel for making electricity.

In most states, however, landfills will be the main method of trash disposal for many years. In Virginia, the city of Virginia Beach extended the life of a landfill by making a mountain out of it. Mt. Trashmore, as it is called, is only 80 feet high but looms above the surrounding flat land. It is made up of 400,000 tons of solid wastes and 280,000 tons of soil. The trash represents five years of wastes from Virginia Beach and two years' worth from nearby Norfolk.

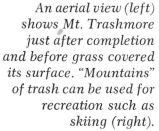

An aerial view (left) shows Mt. Trashmore just after completion and before grass covered its surface. "Mountains" of trash can be used for recreation such as skiing (right).

Like all landfills, Mt. Trashmore is expected to give off odors and to settle unevenly for a time. But its surface is covered with grass. The city has built a soap box derby ramp and has plans for a 10,000-seat amphitheater and an observation tower. The earth used in the landfill was dug from nearby land, and the resulting excavation has been filled with water and is used as a recreation lake. Its waters are tested regularly to see if there is any contamination from the buried wastes.

The city of Virginia Beach will deposit its next 15 to 20 years' trash in another, larger landfill "mountain." A landfill ski hill is being built in Riverview, Michigan. New York City may extend the life of some of its landfills by making a series of rolling hills. Other cities are considering this idea. But Charles S. Kiley, director of the Mt. Trashmore project, admits that such "high-rise landfills" are no permanent solution to solid waste problems. "They eventually are subject to space limitations, too," he said. "Technology will have to advance—through recycling or some other way—to the point where we don't need landfills at all."

The trash collected in cities and towns is only part of the solid waste problem. Many tons of cans, bottles, papers, and other trash are scattered over land and water as litter. People leave litter just about everywhere they visit—especially along roadsides, on beaches, and in parks, but also on remote mountaintops and even on the moon.

Litter, landfills, and city wastes are in the news more and more these days. They are the major subjects of this book. However, wastes from cities make up only about 8 percent of the solid wastes produced in the United States each year. The nation also produces 2.3 billion tons of agricultural wastes and 1.7 billion tons of mining wastes annually.

These wastes are piling up or gradually decaying out in the countryside, and they haven't received much attention. But the problems of air and water pollution they cause will soon demand attention and solutions. The

Crowded together in a feedlot, cattle produce many tons of manure.

agricultural wastes include manure and used bedding. They also include the remains of animals slaughtered for meat, of vegetables and fruits that have been canned or frozen, and of harvested crops, including timber.

Meat animals used to be raised on family farms, and their body wastes were usually spread on fields as fertilizer. Now many farmers find it cheaper and easier to use commercial fertilizer. Also, most beef cattle and hogs are today fattened by the thousands in areas called feedlots. Ten thousand steers in a feedlot produce 260 tons of manure a day. A poultry farm with 100,000 chickens may produce five tons of droppings a day. Of course, a lot of this waste is water which evaporates into the air. But many tons of solid materials are left. Some of it washes into streams and lakes where it is a major source of pollution.

Unlike manure and other agricultural wastes, mining wastes do not decay. They pile up near mines and at smelters, where metals and minerals are removed from the

Drawing by Robt. Day; © 1973 The New Yorker Magazine, Inc.

ore. Mining wastes are ugly. They cover many acres of land, and usually no plants can grow where they have been dumped. Rain washes chemicals from the wastes into streams, killing fish and other water animals for miles downstream.

The problems of solid wastes are great and growing. Solid wastes are a double waste. Not only do they take up space, destroy wild areas, and cause pollution, but the wastes we toss away each day are also valuable. Dumps and landfills are full of treasure. There is paper that can be made into new paper products, glass that can be made into new glass products, garbage that can be changed into a kind of fertilizer. There is also aluminum, steel, copper, and other metals, including silver and gold. No wonder trash is now being called "urban ore."

There is hope that all of the valuable materials in solid wastes can someday be recycled—either used again in the same form or made into a new product. But that day seems far away. Right now the problems of solid wastes are as complex and messy as the contents of a garbage truck.

chapter 2
return or throw away?

In 1973, the solid wastes from cities alone added up to 250 million tons, according to a study by the National League of Cities and the United States Conference of Mayors. Included in this annual mountain of trash were 28 billion bottles, 48 billion cans, 4 million tons of plastic, 30 million tons of paper, 100 million tires, and over 3 million cars.

For the whole country, these totals were even higher. And the amount of trash increases each year, partly because the number of people is increasing but also because each person throws away more trash each year. It has been estimated that by 1980 each person will be throwing away 7.5 pounds of solid wastes each day.

A nation has to be wealthy to be this wasteful, and it seems that the amount of trash produced is one measure of a country's wealth. In India, each person throws away about 200 pounds of waste in a year. Every person in the United States throws away about ten times that much— more than a ton.

The growing amount of trash in the United States contains more and more packaging each year. If you keep track of what you throw away, you will find that a lot of it is packaging. Cans, bottles, boxes, jars, cartons, bags, wrappings—all are packages. They are designed to protect and identify some product, and they usually aren't considered worth keeping. So 90 percent of all packaging is thrown out.

Packaging in trash represents huge amounts of paper, glass, metals, and plastics. It also makes up most of the litter scattered over the countryside.

Most items in "bubble packs" don't need to be packaged at all.

Packaging is sometimes vital—when it protects foods from spoiling, for example. And packaging is convenient when it protects products from damage or makes them easier to carry. But products are often packaged in a way that makes it difficult or impossible to reuse the container. Some packages are made of plastics that may cause serious pollution problems if they are burned. And a lot of packaging is simply unnecessary.

One example of unnecessary packaging is the "bubble pack," in which a small toy, piece of hardware, or other product is surrounded by a piece of cardboard and a bubble of plastic. Most of these items don't need any packaging at all. And the combination of materials—cardboard and plastic—makes it difficult to recycle either one.

Packaging has become a big industry. According to industry forecasts, by 1980 people in the United States will be spending $50 billion for 85 million tons of packaging. And, unless there is drastic change by then, we will throw away most of that packaging and spend more than a billion dollars to get rid of it.

Companies within the packaging industry compete with one another. Each tries to come up with new kinds of packages that will appeal to people, increase sales, and add to the company's profits. Whether the new package is good for the environment is usually not considered.

Container manufacturers say that people demand convenient packages and throwaway containers. But the situation is not that simple. How much of this "demand" is real and how much has been created by advertising paid for by the manufacturer? There is no way to tell. Scientists who study human behavior, however, believe that a lot of container advertising plays upon a basic urge of most people to make life easier for themselves. Encouraged by advertising, people begin buying throwaway containers and discover that they are less trouble than returnables. Throwing away containers becomes a habit. And there is no advertising that tells people that they pay more for beverages in throwaways or that they pay extra taxes to dispose of throwaways in trash and litter.

People have become so accustomed to throwaway containers that they don't realize how much more expensive they are. For example, soft drinks in throwaway bottles cost 30 percent more than in returnable bottles. And if the cost of litter pickup, trash hauling, landfills, energy use, and other expenses of throwaway disposal were added to the purchase price, people would discover the true cost of packaging convenience. It is tremendously expensive.

Soft drinks were once sold only in returnable bottles. A deposit was paid for the use of each bottle. The deposit was refunded when the bottle was returned to the store. The empty bottles were picked up from stores by soft drink companies, washed, refilled, resealed with a cap, and returned to stores for sale. Bottles used to make an average of 40 trips between the soft drink bottlers and consumers.

The story of how people changed from using returnable bottles to using mostly throwaway containers is a good example of the way many environmental problems begin. It also shows that solutions to solid waste problems will not be easy.

The switch from returnable containers to throwaways *did not* begin with crowds of angry people picketing beverage companies, demanding more convenient packag-

Once, nearly all soft drinks were sold in returnable bottles; now many stores sell only the more expensive throwaway containers.

ing. It began when the steel industry looked for new markets in the late 1940s and early 1950s. Together with the can companies, the steel makers decided that there might be a big market for steel cans. Suppose, for example, that people could be persuaded to stop using returnable bottles, which at that time made 40 round trips. Instead people would buy (and throw away) 40 steel cans!

Throwaway cans were successful and began to affect the sales of returnable bottles. So glass manufacturers decided to compete with the can companies. They began selling and advertising their own throwaways—"no deposit–no return" bottles.

The advertising of throwaways was aimed not only at consumers but also at store owners and managers. They were urged to switch to throwaways in order to save storage space and the labor needed to handle returnable bottles. Years of advertising have had an effect on people's buying habits. In 1958, nearly all soft drinks were sold in returnable bottles; by 1976 only an estimated 32 percent will be in returnables. During the same period the amount of beer sold in returnable bottles will have dropped from 58 percent to 20 percent.

Returnable bottles are still available in most cities. The national average of round trips between bottler and consumer, however, has dropped to 15. Returnable bottles are used more by people who live in suburbs than by city people. City shoppers often travel on foot and buy small quantities of beverages. City food stores are usually small and have little storage space for empty bottles. Suburban shoppers usually travel by car and buy large quantities of beverages. They find returnable bottles more convenient than most city people do. Large suburban stores also have more storage space for empty bottles.

Today, returnable bottles make about eight trips between bottlers and consumers in Chicago. They make fewer trips in New York City. Recently a company sold 14.4 million returnable 16-ounce bottles of soft drinks in New York City. Buyers had to pay a nickel deposit on each bottle. Some of the bottles were returned, cleaned, refilled, and sold again. But within a year 11 million bottles had disappeared. People had apparently thrown them away. If someone had managed to rescue all of those bottles, unbroken, from trash cans and turned them in for the deposit refund, he would have received $550,000.

As the use of throwaways has increased, so has the amount of litter. It costs four times as much to collect a ton of litter as it does to collect a ton of garbage. Litter mars the beauty of parks, beaches, and roadsides. And litter sometimes causes automobile accidents, as cars hit junk in the road or swerve to avoid it. In one year the state of Texas alone reported 1,068 litter-caused accidents, with 21 people killed.

During the 1950s, citizens and government officials began blaming container manufacturers for the increase in litter and rising costs of litter cleanup. As a result, in 1953 the can and bottle makers joined with the United States Brewers Association and the National Soft Drink Bottlers Association to form an organization called Keep America Beautiful, Inc. It is a sort of anti-litter organization. It advertises the idea that "people cause pollution." Its advertisements blame litter on people, not on the industries that make and sell throwaway containers.

Besides supporting Keep America Beautiful, Inc., container makers also produce advertisements and pamphlets giving their view of the litter problem. They frequently use figures from a "National Study of Highway Litter," which was paid for by Keep America Beautiful, Inc. The study covered parts of several highways in 29 states. It showed that nearly 60 percent of all litter was paper, while 15 percent was beer and soft drink cans, and 5 percent was beer and soft drink bottles. The results of this study seemed

Bottles and cans are the most noticeable litter along roads.

to show that throwaway cans and bottles are a rather small part of highway litter.

The accuracy of this study has been questioned. It seems that the study was conducted in the winter and spring, when people were drinking more hot liquids like coffee than cold soft drinks and beer. Also, the figures were based on the *number of pieces* picked up along roads. Figured this way, a gum wrapper or napkin was considered to be as important as a can or bottle.

Studies based on the size or volume of items found in litter give a more accurate picture of the makeup of trash we notice along roadsides and elsewhere. The Oregon State Highway Division made such a study in 1971. It showed that cans made up 40 percent of the volume of all litter. Bottles made up 22 percent, while the remaining 38 percent was made up of paper, plastic, and other materials.

Recently, governments in many cities and some states have considered laws that would encourage the use of returnable containers. Some of these laws have been established. In Bowie, Maryland, for example, a deposit is required on all beverage containers. In 1972, Oregon passed a similar law. A refund must be paid on all beer, malt, and soft-drink containers that are returned. Store owners pay the refund if they sell the brand and size of container brought in for refund. The refund is five cents a container, except for a refund of two cents on a standard-sized returnable beer bottle sold in Oregon.

The refund values are clearly marked on all beverage containers. Although there is no official deposit required on containers, dealers add the cost of the refund to the selling price. People can get refunds for empties from stores or from redemption centers that have been set up around the state.

Studies by the Oregon State Highway Division show that roadside litter has declined since the law took effect. Vermont has also established a law that favors the use of returnable bottles, and other states, cities, and counties are considering similar laws. Supporters of such laws believe that this is an effective way of reducing litter and solid wastes. It also encourages people to end their "use it once and throw it away" attitude.

Laws which encourage the use of returnable bottles are, of course, opposed by container manufacturers, steel makers, and glass manufacturers. They want people to keep buying throwaways. Through advertising and other efforts, the container industry encourages people to return throwaways to recycling centers, where the containers can then be melted down to form new containers or other products.

This is one kind of recycling. But so is the use of returnable bottles, which can be refilled again and again. In 1973, Dr. Bruce M. Hannon, an engineer at the University of Illinois, Urbana, made a study of the energy used in these two kinds of recycling. He calculated the amount of energy used to get raw materials for making returnable bottles and throwaway containers. He also figured out the amounts of energy used to make cans, bottles, bottle caps, to fill containers with beverages, and to transport them.

The Oregon State Highway Division studied roadside litter before and after passage of the state's "bottle" law in 1972. The amount of litter declined sharply after the law took effect.

NO DEPOSIT
NO RETURN

BORN CIRCA 1935
DIED IN OREGON
SEPT. 30, 1972

MAY IT RUST IN PEACE

Dr. Hannon found that use of returnable bottles requires much less energy than throwaway bottles or cans. Comparing 16-ounce bottles, he found that throwaways required the use of 4.4 times the energy of returnables. And 12-ounce cans used 2.9 times as much energy as similar-sized returnable bottles. Dr. Hannon's study showed that a complete change to use of returnable bottles would reduce the energy now used by beverage industries by 55 percent. People would also save an estimated $1.4 billion each year by using the cheaper returnable bottles. Dr. Hannon concluded that "from dollar-cost and energy-cost standpoints, returnable bottles are preferable to cans or throwaway bottles."

Can and bottle makers, along with the steel and glass industries, have grown and prospered through the use of throwaways. If everyone began using returnable bottles, these industries would make fewer bottles and their business would suffer. Some workers might lose their jobs. Unemployment might rise for a time in communities where container industries are located. These communities might also lose tax revenue.

For the nation as a whole, however, the use of returnable bottles would have many good effects, including savings in energy and in the costs of cleaning up litter. Also, the jobs lost in one industry would be gained in another. Losses of jobs in the can and bottle industries would be more than offset by increases of jobs in bottling plants and

Throwaway containers are a huge waste of energy and resources.

stores. According to a recent University of Illinois study, a change from throwaway containers to returnable bottles in that state would cause an increase of 6,500 jobs.

However, a national change back to returnable bottles could have some bad effects on the environment. Returnable bottles must be washed before they are refilled. Detergents and about eight gallons of water are used to clean each case of bottles. The beer and soft drink industries would use and pollute more water if they changed to returnable bottles. However, pollution control devices are available to clean water before it leaves bottling plants.

The problem of throwaway containers and other packaging is only part of the total solid waste mess. But it illustrates how complex solid waste problems can be. An end to the use of throwaway containers will require great changes in industries and in the attitudes and behavior of people. Solutions to the costly and growing problems of the "Third Pollution" will not come easily.

chapter 3
rescuing resources

"Trash is Cash."

Use of this slogan is one way in which community recycling organizations urge people to stop throwing away valuable materials. Since 1970, thousands of recycling centers have been set up all over the United States and Canada. Most them began as volunteer efforts and still depend on volunteer labor. Some centers have been taken over by community governments. Some have closed.

No actual recycling goes on at recycling centers. Waste and scrap materials are merely collected there and then taken to paper dealers, glass manufacturers, or scrap metal dealers. If these markets can be found and continue through the years, a community recycling center may meet its expenses. Very few centers make a profit. And many communities have collected great amounts of material only to find that there is no nearby market for it.

One successful recycling effort takes place in the village of Briarcliff Manor, New York. In 1970, a group of high school students approached the village government with the idea of starting a recycling center. Volunteers ran the

31

center for a time, then the village took over. There are only 6,500 people in the village, and it is handy for most of them to bring cans and bottles to big storage bins near the post office. The village's sanitation trucks also make a house-to-house pickup of newspapers and magazines once a month.

The village gets some money by selling the bottles, cans, magazines, and newspapers. It also saves money because it disposes of less solid waste, and thus pays less money at the county landfill, which charges a dumping fee of about $7.50 a ton.

"When you're finished, can I have the empty bottle?"
Drawing by B. Tobey; © 1971 The New Yorker Magazine, Inc.

In Briarcliff Manor and all over North America there are families and individuals who try their best not to throw away valuable materials. A family of seven living near Rochester, New York, throws out only twelve pounds of waste a week and helps recycle about five tons of their trash each year. Thousands of people devote several hours a week in volunteer work at recycling centers. But the facts are that many of these centers have closed, and that the value of this kind of effort has been exaggerated.

There's an old saying about celery—you use more energy chewing it than you get from digesting it. Something like this can be said of most recycling centers. Consider this scene at a recycling center, observed many times by Michigan naturalist Christopher Letts:

"Mrs. Rich pulls up in her Super Polluter 8. She leaves the engine running, so the car will stay air conditioned, and proudly unloads a bag or two of bottles and jars. She says that she wasn't sure whether labels had to be removed [usually they do not], so she ran the containers through the electric dishwasher twice to get them off. Then she drives her Super Polluter home, feeling good about having done something to better our environment.

"She *did* help reduce solid waste and recycle glass. But in the process she used some of the earth's limited supply of gasoline, and polluted water by using the dishwasher. She also added to air pollution by driving the car, and by using electricity, which was probably produced by burning coal. I'm not sure that the environment can stand many more of such helpers."

It is interesting that container manufacturers support local recycling efforts, mostly through advertisements which urge people to recycle cans and bottles. As one company official said, "It's true that it's cheaper for us to buy full-page ads than to face legislation banning non-returnable beverage containers."

These advertisements often suggest that local recycling efforts can have an important national effect on reducing solid wastes and recycling materials. They do not. During 1971 more than 700 million aluminum cans were recycled, but that was only 3.7 percent of the cans manufactured that year. In the same year 1.5 billion steel cans were recycled. That was just 2.3 percent of the number made. And according to the Glass Container Manufacturers Institute, 912 million bottles were recycled, but that was just 2.6 percent of the total number made in one year.

Even so, most experts on solid waste problems are pleased with community recycling centers and give them whatever support they can. Their greatest value seems to be that of educating people. Newspaper publicity about recycling centers has helped make millions of people aware of the value of the stuff they throw away. About recycling centers, Thomas F. Williams of the Environmental Protection Agency's Office of Solid Waste Management Programs in Washington, D.C., said, "They're not economically viable, but I'm doing all I can to keep them afloat because I think they're a good reminder that we've got a problem. . . . I don't think it will take very many years for industry to have to start doing things to back up the claims they are making now in response to all the citizen interest in the recycling of solid wastes."

Fewer than three out of every hundred glass containers are recycled; the rest are thrown away.

"I'm still reading it. When I'm finished, then *you can recycle it."*
Drawing by Modell; © 1974 The New Yorker Magazine, Inc.

Recycling of some materials has gone on for many years, most of it by scrap dealers. They make up an $8 billion industry in the United States. (It is usually called the "secondary materials" industry.) Scrap dealers collect or buy scrap metal, glass, paper, fabric, and other materials from industries and businesses, then sell it to manufacturers. In this way they recycle 18 percent of all the aluminum produced, 50 percent of the copper and brass, 50 percent of the lead, and 19 percent of the paper.

The percent recycled depends directly on the value of the material. Very little gold is tossed out. Recently silver has become scarce, and many photographic laboratories have installed devices which trap silver left over from film processing. It used to wash down drains with waste water.

Scrap dealers seldom get materials that would end up in

a landfill, so their efforts do not really affect the growing
solid waste crisis. It is too costly for them to "mine" the
trash in dumps and landfills, although that may be economical someday. The amounts of metals, glass, and other
materials handled by community recycling centers are also
too small to have much of an effect on reducing solid
wastes. But until some better solutions are found, cities

*The scrap industry already recycles great amounts of some
metals; here are steel fragments from 30,000 automobiles.*

are doing the best they can to stave off the solid waste crisis.

Some communities are trying to reduce their solid waste load by having citizens separate newspapers from other wastes. The towns then sell the newspapers for recycling and save landfill space. The Hackensack Meadowlands Development Commission has alerted the 118 New Jersey communities that use its landfill that they will have to find ways to recycle newspapers. In the future, communities may have to insist that citizens separate trash even more. Each family might have several containers—for metals, glass, paper, garbage, and other materials. This would be a much more effective, though unpopular, way of recycling wastes than volunteer recycling centers.

A few cities have tried to make compost out of some of their wastes. Compost is a mixture of partly decayed organic matter such as paper and garbage. It can be used

At a composting plant (left), solid wastes are shredded before magnets remove the iron and steel. After processing, the dry compost is put into bags for sale at garden supply stores.

as a low quality fertilizer, a mulch, or a conditioner which improves the texture of soil. Many communities make compost from dead leaves they collect from homes in the fall. The compost is used to enrich the soil in city parks and is sold or given away to gardeners and home owners.

Compost from solid wastes is used widely in Europe. In the Netherlands, one sixth of all solid waste is converted into compost. So far, composting has not been very popular in the United States. Recently, two private composting plants near Houston, Texas, were forced to close because of odors and a lack of markets for their product. It seems

Compost from solid wastes might be used to restore strip-mined land.

that people would rather buy peat moss and other materials that serve many of the same purposes than compost. There is doubt that composting will ever help much to reduce the huge volume of waste in North America.

The idea of composting is attractive, though, because it usually begins with some separation of metals, glass, and other inorganic materials. Ideally, these materials can then by recycled. And compost is not dumped but is used to replenish the soil. Compost may yet play a part in the battle against solid wastes, if a big market for the end product can be developed.

One suggested use of compost is to help improve barren areas left after land has been strip mined. It might also be spread along steep roadsides and hills, to help prevent erosion. In a recent two-year study, in Florida, compost made from solid wastes was spread among young trees. The compost itself did not have any effect, good or bad, on the growth of pine seedlings during that period. It did, however, help hold moisture in the sandy soil.

Mixed with chemical fertilizer, compost from solid wastes might be an attractive product for home gardeners. Although about 25 composting plants have been built in the United States (one run by a company called Good Riddance, Incorporated), only four were operating in 1973.

Many cities may turn to incinerators as a way out of the crisis caused by disappearing landfill space. Incinerators are expensive to build and become even more expensive when they have to be improved to meet rising air quality standards. They reduce the volume of wastes that are put in landfills, however, and they can also be used to produce energy.

Shredded trash (above) can be used to make electricity. At a Union Electric Power plant (right) iron and steel are removed from the trash magnetically, then trucked to a steel company.

Most city trash has a fuel value about half that of coal. It can be burned to make steam and electricity. Trash as a source of energy has an advantage over some kinds of oil; it contains little sulfur and therefore does not produce much sulfur dioxide, a serious air pollutant.

For many years incinerators in Europe have made use of the heat energy produced by burning refuse. Now the idea is being studied and adopted in the United States. In 1973, the city of New York began to investigate a plan for burning some of its garbage to make electricity. Chicago and Atlanta already have incinerators that burn trash and produce steam which can then be used to make electricity. The Union Electric Power Company of St. Louis burns about one part shredded trash to every nine parts of coal in one of its furnaces. By 1977, the company expects to use all of the solid waste from the St. Louis area as fuel for generating electricity.

43

Agricultural wastes may someday be used as a source of energy. When manure and other organic wastes decay, they give off natural gas (methane). The Combustion Power Company of California is working on a turbine engine, fueled by animal wastes, which will produce electricity. And a British inventor drives a car powered by methane gas from chicken and pig droppings.

Wastes can also be changed into fuels by a process called pyrolysis. The wastes are put in a chamber that contains little or no air, then are heated to about 500 degrees Centigrade. The trash is reduced to a variety of materials: charcoal, minerals, metals, and a mixture of gases and oils. The metals and minerals can be recycled, and the charcoal, gases, and oils can be used as fuels.

The United States Bureau of Mines has developed a pyrolysis process in which trash is heated under great pressure. This produces less charcoal and more oil than other pyrolysis methods. The charcoal produced is used to fuel the process. Nearly all of the oil remains to be sold. Several companies have developed pyrolysis methods which are being tested in pilot plants. The city of Baltimore, Maryland, plans to build a pyrolysis plant that will take in a thousand tons of waste daily. Gas produced by pyrolysis will be used to heat water, producing steam. The steam will be sold to an electric company and used to make electricity.

City refuse contains many materials that will not burn but can be recycled. Sometimes these valuable resources can be removed before incineration, sometimes after. A study of incinerators in Washington, D.C., showed that the residues were made up of 17 percent "tin" cans (which

ONE TON OF REFUSE YIELDS

Char Residue
154–230 lb.

Tar and Pitch
½–5 gal.

Light Oil
1½–2 gal.

Ammonium
Sulfate
18–25 lb.

Liquor
80–133 gal.

Gas
11,000–17,000
cu. ft.

CONVERSION OF MUNICIPAL REFUSE
TO USABLE PRODUCTS BY PYROLYSIS

Pyrolysis of solid wastes produces a variety of fuels.

are really steel coated with tin); 11 percent iron and steel; 2 percent other metals; 44 percent glass; 2 percent ceramics, stones, and bricks; 9 percent partly burned organic matter; and 15 percent ash.

Today there is great interest in incinerators or other waste treatment plants that are equipped for "resource recovery." One of the systems of this kind was developed by the United States Bureau of Mines. Magnets and

45

screens of different sizes are used to separate such materials as iron and glass. It was discovered that colored glass can be separated from clear glass. Brown and green glass contain iron, so a powerful magnet can pick them up.

Other sorting systems are being developed and tested. One common type uses a sort of wind tunnel. Dry, shredded trash is dropped into the tunnel. The heaviest objects, mostly metals, are carried the shortest distance; lightweight objects are carried the farthest. Another system, being studied by the Franklin Institute of Philadelphia, uses a paddle wheel. Shredded trash is dropped onto the rotating wheel. The paddles "bat" the pieces of trash varying distances. Metal and glass land farthest from the wheel, and paper, plastic, and foil land the closest.

In 1971, the town of Franklin, Ohio, began to operate a resource recovery plant which has attracted a lot of attention. Franklin is a small town, but it received financial help from the federal government and from the Black Clawson Company, which designed and built the plant. Officials from cities all over the world visit Franklin to see this resource recovery plant in action.

The plant takes in 50 tons of wastes in an eight-hour day. The refuse is mashed up with water, forming a slurry. This takes place in a machine called a Hydrapulper. The Hydrapulper ejects most metal, including tin cans. The metal passes through a magnetic separator, which removes iron and steel objects for recycling.

This part of the Black Clawson plant in Franklin, Ohio, removes glass from shredded trash and sorts it by color.

46

Meanwhile, the slurry is put into a machine called a Liquid Cyclone, which spins the wastes around at great speed. The heavier objects spin out of this machine. After drying, these objects pass by magnets, where the last of the iron and steel is plucked out. The remaining materials can be separated into three groupings by weight. Aluminum and plastics make up the lightest part; the middle fraction is almost pure glass; and the heaviest part is metals such as copper, brass, and bronze. Nearly all of these materials can be recycled.

The material left in the Liquid Cyclone is mostly paper but also includes rubber, cloth, food wastes, dirt, and fine bits of glass. These wastes are separated from the paper

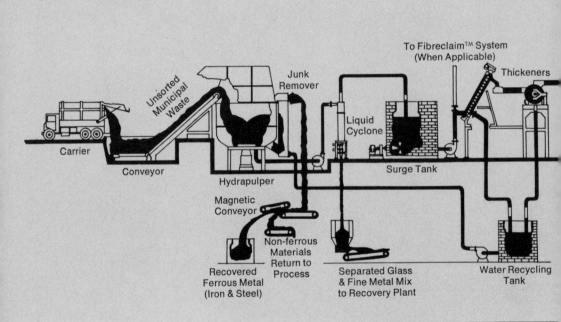

fibers as the slurry passes through a series of screens. The paper is sold to a nearby asphalt roofing company, where it is made into roofing felt.

The organic leftovers are dried and burned, so, in a sense, the Franklin plant is a kind of incinerator. However, it recovers more resources than any other waste treatment plant now working. It recovers about half of the paper fibers that are fed into it, and may be improved to recover more.

The town receives about $95,000 a year from sale of the recovered resources. The Black Clawson Company estimates that a plant taking in a thousand tons of trash a day would cost almost $3000 a day to operate. In one day it

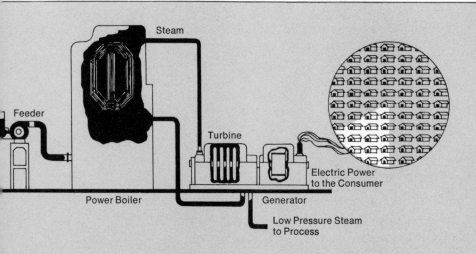

HOW THE BLACK CLAWSON HYDRASPOSAL SOLID WASTE RECYCLING PLANT WORKS

A typical trash can is full of "treasure"—if only reliable markets can be found for the recycled resources.

would produce 370 tons of recycled resources worth $8,600.

Franklin has found a market for all of the resources it recovers, but the same kind of plant in another area might not be able to sell some of these materials. The engineering director of the Black Clawson Company warns: "A city should have customers already lined up before it goes ahead with waste recycling. If all cities had similar systems, they'd have to burn much of the paper they produced."

Sad but true. At resource recovery plants and at volunteer recycling centers, people have discovered that they sometimes can't get rid of the valuable materials they have collected. Sometimes transportation costs are so great that a manufacturer cannot afford to buy and ship materials collected for recycling. Sometimes the quality of the materials is poor, and their use is limited. So far, this is the case with paper fibers from resource recovery plants. The fibers are mixed with bits of plastic, and this prevents their use in many paper products. Finally, even when markets can be found, they can't always be relied upon. The main market for recycled paper fibers is in products like roofing felt, used in home building. But the construction industry varies over the years—sometimes many homes are built, sometimes few are built—and the need for roofing felt varies with it.

However, trash keeps coming in a steady stream, day after day. A resource recovery plant needs reliable markets for its products. Finding and developing markets for resources from trash is one of the most challenging tasks facing the people who are trying to solve solid waste problems.

chapter 4
paper and plastics

Paper makes up about half of the volume of solid wastes collected by cities and towns in North America. It represents great disposal problems—and great recycling opportunities.

About 98 percent of the paper used in the United States is made from wood fibers. But not all of this fiber comes directly from the trunks of trees. Twenty-two percent comes from wastepaper. Twenty-three percent comes from sawmill wastes, such as sawdust, wood chips, and scraps.

According to the paper industry, in 1971, people in the United States used 59 million tons of paper and paperboard (cardboard). Thirteen million tons were recycled; 7 million tons remained in use as books and building materials; 4 million tons were burned in fireplaces or flushed down toilets; and 35 million tons became part of the solid waste mess.

In incinerators and some dumps, paper is usually

People in the United States use nearly 60 million tons of paper and paper products each year.

burned. In landfills, it gradually decays. Paper, like other once-living substances, is biodegradable—it decays, or breaks down, with the help of fungi and bacteria. The decay of paper and garbage is the main cause of settling in landfills.

Recycling of paper has gone on for centuries. During World War II, about 40 percent of the paper used in the United States was recycled. Since then the amount recycled has stayed near 20 percent. Several other countries recycle much more. Japan reuses nearly half of its paper.

According to the United States Environmental Protection Agency, the recycling of paper saves a lot of energy. Making paper from wastepaper uses 70 percent less energy than making it from wood. In 1970, the National Academy of Sciences recommended that by 1985 the United States should be recycling 35 percent of the paper used annually. Other government reports suggest that 50 percent recycling can be reached by that year. Reaching either of these goals, like reaching other goals in recycling, is more easily said than done.

One problem is that wood fibers undergo many changes as they are made into various paper products and then used. About 80 percent of wood fibers used in the United States are produced by using chemicals to dissolve lignin, the substance in wood that holds the fibers together. These fibers are long, strong, and can be easily bleached white. The remaining 20 percent of wood fibers used are quite different. They are ground from logs that are held against a whirling grindstone. These groundwood fibers still contain lignin, which eventually causes the paper to turn yellow and become brittle. So groundwood fibers are used in

54

products where permanence is not important, such as paper for newspapers and magazines.

The fibers undergo further changes before they finally become paper products. Clay may be added to make a paper especially smooth. Dyes and pigments add color. If paper is made into an envelope, part of it is coated with glue. The envelope may also have a cellophane window. All of these changes make recycling difficult. The paper collected from homes, stores, and offices is a mixture of different fibers, colors, and coatings. It is usually mixed with food wastes, rubber bands, staples, and carbon paper.

This mixture is a mess, and paper mills don't want it. Most of the paper being recycled comes from other sources. The kinds of paper currently being recycled are mostly corrugated boxes, newspapers, mixed papers from office buildings, and high quality wastepaper from printing plants. Paper mills also use envelope trimmings and tabulating cards. Almost all of the wastepaper that is easy to collect and sort is already being recycled.

Paper companies have recently begun to advertise that they recycle paper and that they are helping to solve solid waste problems. In most cases, however, these companies have not increased the amount of paper they recycle. Many companies recycle only the wastes from their own manufacturing process, which never leave the mill. In the past, it seemed wise for paper companies not to mention that their products were made partly from wastes. Now it is considered good business to boast about it.

Many of the paper products you buy contain some recycled fibers. Corrugated boxes are made into new corrugated boxes and wallboard. Newspapers are made into egg cartons, corrugated boxes, wallboard, and newsprint (the paper used for newspapers). Office wastes are made into roofing felt, shoe boxes, and tablet backs. Every time you buy something in a gray box, you have a container that was probably once newspaper. It is gray because of the black ink remaining on the fibers.

In recent years the demand for old newspapers has sometimes exceeded the supply. In 1971, a "critical shortage" of used newspapers in the East and Midwest was reported by the American Paper Institute. Of course, dumps and landfills are overflowing with newspapers, but at this time it is not economical for paper dealers to separate newspapers from other trash.

One company in the United States makes newsprint from old newspapers. The Garden State Paper Company

Many corrugated boxes (left) are recycled. The recycling of newspapers (right) will increase as the demand for wood fibers grows.

has plants in Chicago, Los Angeles, and Garfield, New Jersey. It removes the ink from about 400,000 tons of newspapers each year. The newsprint it produces costs a little less than paper made from trees. So far, however, recycled newspapers provide only about 5 percent of the newsprint used in the United States.

It will probably take many years before more newspaper is recycled into newsprint. Some newspaper publishing companies own large tracts of forest land and run their own paper mills. The *Los Angeles Times*, for example, has its own paper mills in Oregon. It uses newsprint from these mills even though recycled newsprint is available from a nearby plant of the Garden State Paper Company. Other newspaper publishing companies have long-standing contracts with forest owners and paper mills, and cannot or will not change quickly to another source of newsprint.

Another obstacle to increased recycling of newspapers is the location of paper mills. Many of them are close to their normal supply of wood fibers, far from cities. The greatest amounts of easily collected newspapers are in cities and suburbs, far from most paper mills. Transporting old newspapers to the mills adds to their cost. Railroad freight rates are higher for wastepaper than for the wood—called pulpwood—used to make paper. For example, in the eastern United States, it costs $14 to carry some pulpwood 95 miles by train. It costs $28 to send an equal amount of wastepaper the same distance.

Some paper mills that used to recycle old newspapers and other wastepaper have closed. They were small plants

Freight rates have been lower for pulpwood than for wastepaper.

with old equipment. They could not compete with more modern mills and, in some cases, could not afford the changes needed to meet new air and water pollution standards.

Recycling of wastepaper does produce wastes of its own that must be disposed of. Old newspapers are no great problem; they contain only ink. For some products, the ink doesn't have to be removed at all. When ink is removed, pollution control devices can keep it from spoiling streams and lakes near the paper mill. Other kinds of wastepaper cause more problems. When clay-coated wastepaper is re-

As long as pulpwood is abundant and cheaper to ship than

cycled, a ton of waste sludge is produced for every ton of paper fiber recovered.

Problems like these can and must be solved if more wastepaper is to be recycled. Eventually, there may be a shortage of pulpwood. Should this happen, the value of wood fibers in wastepaper will rise, and greater efforts will be made to recycle them.

Some people claim that recycling paper saves forests from being cut, because 17 trees are used to make a ton of paper. Actually, one big tree can yield several tons of paper. Big trees are normally used for lumber, however,

wastepaper, the recycling of paper is not likely to increase much.

and certain kinds of smaller evergreens are grown for the specific purpose of papermaking. They are cut when they reach the proper size, just as wheat and other crops are harvested when ready. Then the landowner usually plants a new crop of trees. It is true that about 17 of these trees are cut down in order to make a ton of paper. But the trees are replaced. At this time the amount of pulpwood grown is 30 percent greater than the amount cut. However, by 1985 and perhaps sooner, forestry experts estimate, the demand for pulpwood will be greater than the amount growing. Wood fibers going to waste will become more valuable.

The market for recycled paper has increased a little because some organizations, businesses, and governments insist that stationery and other paper they use contain some recycled fibers. New York City was the first city to adopt this policy. In 1971, the General Services Administration, which buys supplies for the federal government, began purchasing paper containing some recycled fibers.

Many politicians and some businesses and organizations use stationery and other printed materials marked "printed on recycled paper." Sometimes the paper is made entirely from recycled fibers, sometimes it is not. If the words "contains recycled fibers" appear, it may mean that the paper is made of as much as 75 percent recycled paper—or much, much less. City and state governments, large organizations, and businesses—all use a lot of paper. The market for recycled paper will grow if more of them use their purchasing power to encourage recycling.

As more recycling is done, the question "How many times can a fiber be reused?" may be answered. Each time a fiber is reused, it becomes shorter. That makes it less desirable for use in such products as paper bags, which must be strong. Paper made with reused fibers tears more easily than paper made from fresh fibers. However, recycled fibers have some advantages. Paper containing them shrinks less and is less apt to curl than paper made entirely from fresh fibers. For some grades of printing paper, recycled fibers are best.

Scientists are investigating ways to reuse wood fibers in products other than paper. They have found that newspapers can be made into fireproof insulation for buildings. Wastepaper can even be made into "wooden" boards. In uses like these, the question of how many times fibers can be recycled does not matter, since the paper is made into a long-lived product.

Recently, scientists working at the United States Army Laboratories in Natick, Massachusetts, found that wastepaper can be used to clean up oil spills. They used a hammermill to break wastepaper down into tiny fragments of wood fibers. The fibers collected 27 times their own weight in oil—much more than straw, clay, or sawdust, the materials often used to clean up oil spills. The oil-soaked paper stayed on the water surface and was easily skimmed off. The scientists reported that oil could be squeezed out and the paper fragments used again. If this method is a success in large-scale tests, it will create a rather small, but very important, new use for wastepaper.

For cities which are planning to burn most of their solid wastes for energy, paper is an important fuel. Depending on the amount of water it contains, wastepaper has 35 to 60 percent of the heating value of coal. Ink,

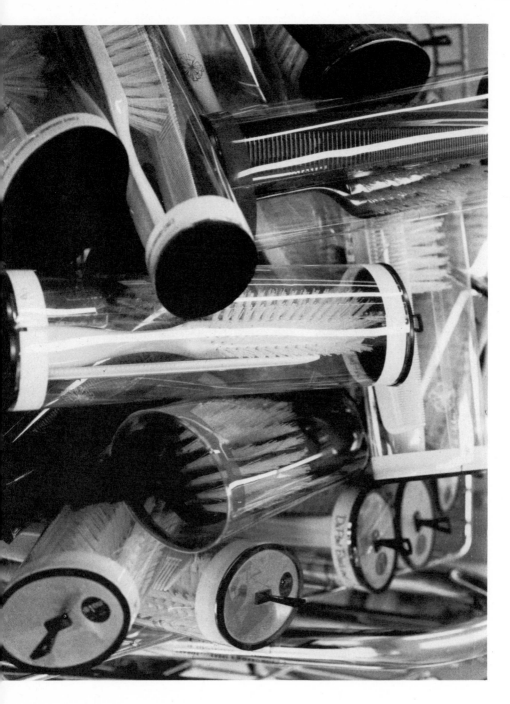

wax, and plastic coatings on paper actually increase its fuel value. In the short run, it seems wise to burn paper for energy and to reduce the burden on landfills. Eventually, however, a shortage of wood fibers for papermaking will probably make it necessary to recycle more and more paper.

Compared with paper, plastics are a very small part of solid wastes. Plastics make up only about 2 percent by weight of the solid wastes collected. But the amount of plastics in trash is growing; by 1980 they are expected to be 3 percent. By volume, of course, these lightweight materials already make up a greater percentage. And the characteristics of plastics make them an especially troublesome part of trash.

Almost 10 million tons of plastics are produced in the United States each year. Over half are polyethylene, used in packaging, molded containers, bottles, and upholstery. About 20 percent are polystyrene, used in dishes, refrigerators, and air conditioners. Polyvinyl chloride is made into such things as phonograph records, curtains, rainwear, and luggage. Polyurethane is used in heat insulation, air filters, and mattress padding.

Plastics have a high fuel value and aid the burning of other trash in incinerators. When polyvinyl chlorides burn, however, hydrochloric acid is given off. It eats away the insides of incinerators. Sometimes the acid escapes into the air. It can be trapped within an incinerator equipped with modern air pollution control devices. Not all incinerators

Increasing amounts of plastics are used in packaging, which is usually discarded soon after purchase.

have such devices, of course. Neither do burning dumps. So a fine mist of hydrochloric acid is produced when trash is burned in such places. It damages buildings, clothes, plants, and perhaps other living things.

So far, no plastic is being recycled from trash. Compared with other items, there isn't very much of it, so recovering great amounts would be a difficult and costly task. Another problem lies in the plastics themselves. They differ enough chemically so that they cannot be melted down together and used to form new products. They have to be sorted and recycled separately. Also, the colors are usually part of the plastic, not like the pigments which coat paper fibers and can be removed. This means that plastic objects taken from trash also have to be sorted by color.

Plastics are a rather small part of all solid waste, but they are a long-lasting problem. They do not decay quickly, as paper and food wastes do. One study showed that polyvinyl chlorides do break down in landfills but will be only half gone after 85 years in the soil.

Six-pack harnesses like this one have caused the death of birds which became tangled in them.

chapter 5
cars, cans, cloth, and glass

The Goodwins wanted to get rid of their car. It had traveled over 100,000 miles and had served them well. But now it seemed beyond repair. So they called auto junkyards and found one that would take it. They were paid nothing for it and had to deliver it themselves. Fortunately, they did not have to pay to have the car towed; it traveled its last few miles under its own power.

Not everyone is so careful about disposing of a car. Many people abandon their cars on the street. About a thousand a week are abandoned in Washington, D.C.; about 1,600 a week are left on the streets of New York City. Perhaps there are litterbugs (people who litter) who, while throwing away gum wrappers and cans, dream of someday tossing away a whole car!

The automobile is certainly one of the most noticeable objects of solid waste. About eight million cars and a million trucks and buses are scrapped each year. Fortunately, only about 15 percent are abandoned. Wrecked or old cars are a source of scrap metal, although many are not used immediately. About 16 million are now in junkyards or "auto graveyards." Another four million are scattered over the countryside, in fields, forests, and small towns.

According to the United States Bureau of Mines, a junked automobile weighing 3,600 pounds is made up of approximately 2,500 pounds of steel, 500 pounds of cast iron, 54 pounds of zinc, 51 pounds of aluminum, and 20 pounds of lead. (The remaining 400 pounds are glass, upholstery, plastic, and other nonmetallic materials.)

Since a car contains great amounts of steel and other metals, it seems at first to be a recycling prize. It is not. The metals in an average car were worth about $56 in 1973. At that time, it cost $51 to separate the metals from the other materials in a car and to transport the metals to market.

Most used cars are sold to auto wreckers who then resell auto parts. There isn't much demand for parts of older cars. By the time an auto wrecker takes an older car apart and has it ready for sale as scrap metal, it may have cost him more than it is worth. So auto wreckers usually pay nothing for older cars. This helps explain why some people abandon their cars.

Governments in some cities and states have taken steps to encourage auto wreckers to clear cars off streets and to discourage people from abandoning cars. In Maryland, for example, there is a $200 fine for abandoning a car. Also, each time a car is sold, the new owner pays a dollar bounty fee to the state. The state uses the money from the bounty fund to pay scrap dealers $10 for each car they process. This system encourages auto wreckers and scrap dealers to seek out and dispose of old cars.

As the price of scrap steel rose in 1974, the stacks of cars in "auto graveyards" began to disappear.

70

Materials in a 1972 American automobile

1	Light steel (less than ⅛-inch thick)	3	Cast iron	7	Molded nylon
2	Heavy iron and steel (greater than ⅛-inch thick)	4	Mineral wool	8	Bakelite plastic
		5	Glass	9	Lead
		6	Activated carbon	10	Stainless steel

11	Asbestos	16	Rubber	21	Polypropylene
12	Copper and brass	17	Polyurethane foam	22	Nylon fabric
13	Aluminum	18	Acrylic	23	ABS plastic
14	Zinc	19	Vinyl plastic	24	Paper
15	Asphalt-like plastic	20	Polyethylene	25	Cotton and jute

Auto wreckers first remove parts which can be resold or easily recycled. The engine and transmission are almost entirely cast iron. Wheels are made of steel. The radiator, generator, and engine wiring are made of copper and brass. There's lead in the battery.

The rest of the car is mostly steel, but it is mixed with other metals, plastics, rubber, glass, and fabrics. Most of this material must be stripped from a car before it can be sold for scrap steel. Auto wreckers used to burn out cars in order to get rid of this material. Laws against air pollution now prevent this in most states. Some auto wreckers have built their own incinerators to burn out cars. The United States Bureau of Mines has developed an inexpensive, smokeless incinerator for this purpose.

After a car leaves an auto junkyard it may be bundled, sheared, or shredded. In a bundling mill the car is squeezed into a cube. Since these cubes still contain some metals and other materials mixed with the steel, they are not as valuable to steel mills as cars that have been sheared or shredded. In the shearing process, flattened cars are chopped into pieces by an enormous blade. In shredding, cars are hammered apart into fist-sized lumps. After shearing or shredding, magnets are used to remove the steel from the other materials.

There are more than a hundred auto shredders in the United States. Shredding is more expensive than other methods, but it produces high-quality scrap steel at a fast rate—up to 60 cars an hour. Shredders are helping to solve the problem of abandoned cars because there are ready markets for steel of the quality they produce.

Shredded and sheared steel from cars is sold mostly to

After an auto is shredded or sheared, the iron and steel are magnetically separated from other materials.

steelmakers in foreign countries. In fact, officials in the scrap metal business say they could not have survived the past dozen years without these markets. This was not always so. Until about 1956, scrap iron and steel from automobiles was easily sold to the United States steel industry. Then the steel industry began to change its way of making steel, from open-hearth furnaces to basic oxygen furnaces, which use smaller amounts of scrap.

The market for auto scrap in the United States practically disappeared. It was at this point that cars began piling up in auto graveyards and being abandoned all over. The auto scrap business survived by selling scrap to foreign steelmakers and to small United States steel mills that use a new electric furnace. This kind of furnace uses lots of scrap iron and steel.

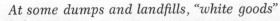

At some dumps and landfills, "white goods"

Steel from old cars is not made into new cars. Recycled steel still contains some copper, and as little as 1 percent copper in steel affects its quality, making it brittle. Scrap steel from cars is usually made into girders for bridges and buildings, or into bars used to reinforce concrete.

Recently, the foreign market for auto scrap has been so good that shredders have begun to reduce the huge backlog of junked cars. Shredders also take in old refrigerators, stoves, and washing machines (called "white goods" in the scrap metal industry). About 21 million of these appliances are discarded each year, and they are made of about 90 percent steel.

Scientists have studied the recycling opportunities in old cars and have found better ways to recover valuable materials. The Bureau of Mines has developed a method

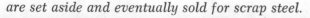

are set aside and eventually sold for scrap steel.

for recovering copper from starters, generators, and other auto parts that are made of copper and iron or steel. The parts are dipped in a bath of molten salt. The copper quickly melts and settles to the bottom, where it is easily drained off. This method recovers about 99 percent of the copper.

Japanese engineers have invented a way of recovering different metals from crushed automobile bodies. The cars travel along a conveyor belt and are baked in a machine called the Carbecue. The temperatures within the Carbecue vary, and different metals melt at different temperatures. First lead, then aluminum, and then copper melt, drip out, and are collected. The iron and steel remain.

One of the most troublesome auto leftovers is the tires. About 100 million are discarded each year. When burned in dumps and incinerators, they produce great clouds of black smoke. Because of this, fewer tires are burned each year, and great numbers are piling up. Fortunately, several uses for old tires have been developed in the past few years.

Pyrolysis of tires yields tar, charcoal, gases, and oils, all of which have some value. A ton of tires produces as much as 140 gallons of oil and 1,500 cubic feet of a gas similar to natural gas. When a mixture of oil and ground-up tires undergoes pyrolysis, a substance called carbon black is produced. This is used to strengthen tire rubber and can be used in making new tires.

This process was developed by the Cities Service Company and the Goodyear Tire and Rubber Company. Goodyear officials estimate that a third of all auto tires scrapped each year could be used as a source of carbon black for new tires. So far, however, the cost of collecting the tires, of removing fabric and wire from them, and of grinding them up makes this process more costly than making tires the old way.

In the 1970s, New York State's Department of Transportation began mixing ground rubber from old tires with the asphalt used to fill cracks and joints in highways and bridges. Four years of tests had shown that the addition of rubber made the asphalt seals last longer. The cost of maintaining highways can be reduced by using this asphalt–rubber mixture. It is estimated that every discarded tire in the United States could be used if all new asphalt contained just 5 percent rubber.

There are potential markets for old tires, but it remains to be seen whether economical ways can be found to recover tires from trash. One advantage of iron and steel is their ability to be separated magnetically from other materials. This vital characteristic makes it possible to recover these metals from trash either before or after it is burned. The city of Atlanta is able to reclaim 99 percent of all steel cans from its incinerator residues. Removing cans before incineration is best, though. During incineration, some copper melts and mixes with the steel in the trash; this makes recycling of both metals more difficult.

The different characteristics of steel and copper are used to advantage by the copper industry, where shredded steel cans are used in the process of recovering copper from its ore. About one to two pounds of cans are used to help produce a pound of copper. During the process, copper collects on the surface of the steel cans. It is later removed. Unfortunately, the cans cannot be used again for copper

At steel mills, tin is removed from steel cans, which are then pressed into bales and moved magnetically to furnaces.

refining or as scrap steel. Each year about 100,000 tons of steel cans are used for this purpose in the southwestern United States, where copper refineries use this process. However, only 4 percent of copper ore in the United States is refined by this method, and the numbers of cans used is only a small part of the annual supply.

Steel companies buy or take back the steel they produced for cans, but they are not usually eager for it. It often comes back to them with tin coating, with lead in the soldered seams, and sometimes with aluminum tops. These substances make the cans unfit for use in the common basic oxygen steel furnace. Economical ways have been found, however, for removing tin from steel cans so that both metals can be recycled. Also, "tin" cans are gradually being replaced by cans coated with chromium or

"Tin" cans are often a mixture of steel, tin, lead, and aluminum, which makes recycling of these metals difficult.

plastic resins, either of which makes cans more acceptable as scrap.

The major obstacle to greater recycling of steel cans is the cost of getting them back to the steel mills. This is much less of a problem with aluminum because it has much higher scrap value. In 1974, aluminum companies were paying about $200 a ton for scrap aluminum—ten times the price paid for steel cans.

Aluminum is very expensive to produce. It is made from bauxite ore, 90 percent of which is imported from foreign countries. Between 13,000 and 18,000 kilowatt-hours of electricity are needed to make each ton of aluminum from bauxite. Three tons of mineral wastes are left over. The recycling of aluminum scrap uses only 2 to 4 percent as much electricity and produces almost no waste. A little aluminum is lost in the process; it takes about 126½ used cans to make 115 new ones.

About a million tons of aluminum are thrown away each year, and aluminum manufacturers are eager to recover much more of it. But it is not easily separated from other trash, as iron and steel are. If a separation method can be found, there is lots of aluminum, still useful, waiting in dumps and landfills. According to Dr. Edwin L. Owen of Pennsylvania State University, it may take about 500 years for an aluminum can lying in a forest to break down into small particles. This is a rough estimate, and a can might break down a century sooner if buried underground. As more and more of the earth's supply of bauxite is mined, the value of existing aluminum will rise. It is not far-fetched to imagine dumps and landfills being mined for aluminum and possibly other materials in the future.

When aluminum cans are recycled, they are first shredded into dime-sized chips (left, above). Fed into a furnace, the chips become molten aluminum, which is poured into molds (left, below). The aluminum is then shipped to a fabricating plant, where it may be pressed into a thin sheet (above), from which new cans are made.

Unlike aluminum, glass is made from cheap and abundant substances—sand, limestone, and soda ash. It costs about a penny for the materials in a pound of glass. Approximately 16 million tons of glass are produced each year in the United States. Two-thirds of this is glass used in containers for beverages, catsup, aspirin, and many other products.

Like aluminum, glass is an easy material to recycle. Waste glass is called cullet, and some has always been used in making new glass. It speeds the melting of the other materials in the glass furnace. Most cullet is scrap from within the manufacturing plant, although people

Glasphalt paving is being tested on at least 15 streets and highways in the United States and Canada.

used to make a living by picking glass from dumps and selling it for cullet. Today, crushed glass, already sorted by color and cleaned, is worth about $20 a ton at the glass plant. The glass industry estimates that cullet can make up 30 percent or more of the raw materials used to make new bottles.

Bottles and jars are the only objects in solid wastes that can be recycled in their original form. However, the glass industry has concentrated on developing ways for using waste glass. It can be used in insulation, bricks, tiles, building blocks, and other construction materials.

One of the most promising uses is "glasphalt," a road-surfacing material. Crushed glass is substituted for crushed gravel and stone, which usually make up about 60 percent of asphalt. The use of glasphalt as a paving material is being tested in several states. Omaha, Nebraska, was the first city to try glasphalt paving. As the city is 400 miles from the nearest market for recycled glass, 300,000 bottles and jars were collected and used to repave parts of a heavily traveled street.

Another possible use of waste glass is to make artificial sand from it. Millions of dollars are being spent to replace sand that is washed away from beaches, especially along the eastern coast of the United States. Most of the sand used so far has been dredged from nearby bays. The sand particles are small; a larger size would be more effective at slowing beach erosion. Waste glass could be ground down to a coarse size that would do a better job, and rough edges could be smoothed so that people would not be cut.

The waste glass is available. People in New York City

throw out about 320,000 tons a year that could be used by nearby shore communities with difficult erosion problems. But there are many obstacles to the process of separating glass from other trash and delivering it in a usable form near beaches.

Bottles and cans as litter, and abandoned cars as a giant form of litter, are in the news a lot. Few people know that there is a growing problem of waste cloth (textiles). Within the textile industry, as much as 500 million pounds of cuttings and clippings and other kinds of unusable and unsalable wastes are produced each year. Another 10 million pounds of discarded cloth is sorted every month, with about 40 percent reused as wiping rags by industry. Most of the rest is thrown away. And finally, there are the textiles that people throw away in their household trash—an

The clothes we wear are often a blend of different fibers, and this makes recycling of fabrics difficult and costly.

estimated 10 million pounds a month. Total textile waste is between 600 and 700 million pounds a year.

A lot of waste cloth used to be recycled. Cotton and wool products were taken apart, spun into yarns, and woven back into cloth. These fibers were also made into rugs and upholstery, used as stuffing in furniture, used as backing for linoleum, and used in the making of fine writing paper. These markets are gradually disappearing. Paper makers turned to wood pulp, linoleum makers began using wood chips, and car makers switched to foam rubber upholstery.

The greatest setback to textile recycling occurred in 1941, when a law called the Wool Labeling Act took effect. It was supported by wool growers and some woolen mills. They wanted to increase their business and lessen competition from recycled wool. Fabrics were labeled "re-used" if made of wool that had once been worn, or "reprocessed" if made from leftover cuttings. This helped people know what they were buying. Once the law took effect, however, advertisements encouraged people to believe that so-called virgin (unused) wool was better than reused or reprocessed wool. The market for recycled wool began to disappear in the United States. For the past twenty years most recycled wool has been exported to Europe. There it is made into clothing which is not labeled "reused" or "reprocessed." Some of these clothes are then sold in the United States. Now, however, Europeans are becoming richer and more wasteful. They discard enough used wool to meet most of the needs of their own woolen mills.

The amount of textiles being recycled has also dropped because of the great variety of fabrics sold today. Most cloth is now made from a blend of fibers. Some fabrics have water repellent finishes, others have flameproof finishes. Separating the different kinds of fabrics from each other has become a difficult and costly job.

Officials of fabric recycling companies are gloomy about the prospects of their industry. The greatest hope seems to lie in teaching people that "new" does not necessarily mean "better." As one official of a textile company said, "We may again return to the 'waste not, want not' era, when people willingly bought serviceable products made from reused materials that often matched the quality of those made from unused materials—and at less cost."

These words apply not just to textiles, but to dozens of other things we buy and use each day.

90

chapter 6
design for recycling

"Drowning in Waste? Vaporize It by Fusion!"

Recently this headline appeared above a newspaper article about an idea for recycling solid wastes. The idea is to use nuclear fusion—the process that produces the sun's energy—to turn wastes into basic raw materials that could be easily recycled. Somewhere near the end of the article it mentioned that fusion may not be a workable process until the year 2000.

Each year there are similar announcements about possible solutions to solid waste problems, large and small: packages that you can eat instead of throw away; old newspapers used as cattle feed; a way of recycling plastic foam from cars. Some ideas are never heard of again. The newspaper articles often fail to mention obstacles which might make the ideas unworkable. Articles like these support a common and foolish notion—that scientists and engineers will find a cheap and easy way to solve just about any problem.

In 1973, the Ford Motor Company announced it had

In newspapers and magazines, the problems of solid waste disposal are finally getting the attention they deserve.

discovered a way of recovering polyurethane foam from automobiles. This plastic foam is used behind instrument panels and in seats. Two hundred million pounds were used in cars made in 1972, and 600 million pounds are expected to be used in 1975. Ford engineers discovered a fairly simple process which melts the foam into the two chemicals from which it is made. The chemicals can then be molded into new foam for new cars or into other products.

So far, so good. But how much will it cost to collect foam from auto wreckers and return it to the foam-manufacturing plants? Once the costs of collecting and transporting the foam are added on, will used foam be able to compete with the price of fresh chemicals?

What seems at first to be a great idea for solving solid waste problems sometimes proves to be unworkable, or may even make matters worse. Since the solid waste mess is partly a result of poor planning or no planning at all, it is important to study possible solutions carefully.

As solid waste problems worsen, people often ask: "How did we get into this mess?" One reason is revealed in Chapter 2: industries, in their efforts to make greater profits and to compete with one another, have encouraged people to be wasteful. Another reason is that the United States government has for many years *discouraged* recycling. Tax laws and freight rates favor the companies that use raw materials. Freight rates set by the Interstate Commerce Commission are sometimes 50 to 100 percent higher for scrap materials than for competing raw materials. Special tax benefits are given to industries that take raw materials such as fuels, ores, and forest products from the land. Environmental groups began trying to change these unfair laws and rates in the early 1970s.

These tax and freight rules may have made sense long ago, when the federal government tried to encourage the development of a new nation. That time is long past. As Jerome Scharf of the National Association of Recycling Industries recently said, "All our laws and regulations were designed for a pioneering, frontier country. Tax advantages were given to mining and timber companies, and that's fine. There are still trees that could be cut and ores that could be mined, but is that the way we want to go, continuing to cut and mine and discard? Or do we want to go toward recovering and reusing our resources?"

This theme was also stated in 1971 by John V. Lindsay, then mayor of New York City, when he spoke at a recycling meeting. "Opposition to recycling," the mayor said, "has become virtually a national policy. It is perhaps inadvertent. But it is surely an environmental mistake. We must end it now."

"Now" takes a while, even though the Environmental Protection Agency also recommended several steps the federal government could take to encourage recycling. In a 1973 report, the agency called for an end to freight rates and tax rules that favor users of raw materials. It also suggested that labeling laws (such as the Wool Labeling Act) be changed; that the federal government should limit the amount of virgin materials in the products it buys;

For years, freight rates have been set so that shipping scrap costs more than shipping an equal amount of raw materials.

that the government should consider new taxes on virgin materials and a system of payments or tax benefits for industries that use recycled materials.

Ideas like these are opposed by the steel, oil, glass, aluminum, beer, soft drink, timber, and container industries. With all of these powerful industries opposed to change, it is not surprising that progress has been slow.

A model of a resource recovery plant built for the state of Delaware. Federal funds are needed to build other pilot plants.

Although the Bureau of Mines has studied some recycling problems for many years, it was not until 1965 that the federal government recognized the growing problem of solid waste. The Solid Waste Disposal Act became law that year. It set up the Bureau of Solid Waste Management, which began to study the problem. In 1970, the bureau became part of the Environmental Protection Agency. In the same year an important law called the Resource Recovery Act was passed. The change of names in the two laws—from "waste disposal" to "resource recovery"—showed that understanding of solid waste problems had also changed.

The Resource Recovery Act authorized the spending of $450 million over a three-year period. Of this amount, more than $220 million was supposed to be given to local communities. They were to use the money to build new waste disposal plants or to set up pilot plants to test resource recovery systems. Some of this money helped make possible the resource recovery plant at Franklin, Ohio.

Most of the money authorized by Congress has not been spent. For example, in fiscal year 1973 (from July 1, 1972 to June 30, 1973) the Act authorized spending $140 million to help build pilot recycling plants. But the Nixon administration wanted to spend only about $20 million, and Congress finally appropriated $15 million. And in 1973, the budget for the Office of Solid Waste Management Programs in the Environmental Protection Agency was cut from $27 million to $5.5 million. The staff was cut by almost two-thirds.

The Resource Recovery Act was supposed to expire on June 30, 1973 but was extended for at least a year. People

concerned about solid wastes know that the law that will eventually replace it could have a great effect on the speed with which solid waste problems are solved. Most experts agree that many millions of federal dollars are needed to help test recycling ideas and to demonstrate workable resource recovery systems.

Other laws have been proposed that aim to help solve solid waste problems in different ways. One would put a special federal tax on any products that end up in solid wastes within ten years of being made. The tax would be a penny a pound. Manufacturers would pay this tax to the federal government, which would then divide the money among the communities which have to dispose of the wastes. A penny a pound equals $20 a ton, which is about what most cities now spend to collect and dispose of wastes.

If this law took effect, manufacturers would add the cost of the tax to their goods. Consumers would pay for the disposal of products as they bought them. The law would also encourage manufacturers to use as little packaging as possible and to design their products so that they could be easily recycled or so that they lasted much longer. Unfortunately, some manufacturers might just switch to lighter materials, such as plastics, unless the law discourages them from doing so.

A law like this would at least help to reveal the real cost of products. Under the present system, each product has hidden costs. Take packaging for instance. You pay

Most packaging is thrown away, and the hidden costs of its disposal will become more and more expensive.

for it when you buy a product. You pay again, through taxes, to have the packaging collected with other trash. And you pay again, though not necessarily with money, when the packaging, along with other wastes, lowers the quality of the environment. Many environmentalists believe that hidden costs should be paid for by manufacturers and those people who choose to buy their products, not by taxes paid by the general public.

The words "too little, too late" describe the federal effort in recycling resources through the year 1974. Several cities and states had to delay building resource recovery plants when expected federal funds were withheld. But with landfill space disappearing, many cities will have to plunge ahead, as best they can, with some other method of waste disposal. Taxes in some communities may rise as the cheap and easy dump-and-landfill era ends. The hidden costs of a throwaway lifestyle will become more noticeable.

Some communities and states have taken the lead in facing solid waste problems. The state of Connecticut has a farsighted program designed to handle all of its wastes. By 1985, it plans to have ten resource recovery centers in different parts of the state. The first one, built in Bridgeport, is expected to recover 72,000 tons of iron and steel, 47,000 tons of glass, 4,000 tons of aluminum, and energy equal to 650,000 barrels of oil, annually. By 1985, the regional plants are expected to provide 11 percent of the state's energy needs. The state of New Jersey is considering a similar plan, with 25 resource recovery plants to be built.

Heavily populated states such as Connecticut and New Jersey have to take these steps. Less populated areas may be able to go on using dumps and landfills for a time. An

100

Aluminum "pull tabs" were designed for convenience,
with no thought given to their effect on the environment.

era of resource recovery systems is definitely coming, but government officials are understandably reluctant to spend millions of dollars on untried systems that may become outdated before they are paid for.

Some help has come from industries which sense that the trash recycling business can be big business. Several

The number of homes built each year affects the market for some products made from recycled materials.

companies have built, or helped build, resource recovery plants. But solid waste is a national problem, and help from the federal government is needed. There are at least two ways in which a new kind of help is needed. One is to develop markets for recycled materials.

In 1972, Samuel J. Hale, an administrator for solid waste programs of the Environmental Protection Agency, said, "It's silly to spend a lot of money developing the technology until you solve the market problem." He added, "The question is no longer whether we should intervene in the market but what form that intervention should take."

Actually, the development of resource recovery plants and of markets should go hand in hand, but little attention has been paid to finding markets. At the Black Clawson plant in Franklin, Ohio, for example, the recovered paper fibers are now sold to a roofing company. In another area there might be no market. But the recovered paper fibers have several potential uses. Identifying these uses and developing markets for them is a vital step in recycling all resources now being tossed out.

There is one other way in which the federal government can help solve solid waste problems. For a long time, people cared only about disposing of wastes; now they are increasingly concerned about recycling. The next logical step is to avoid as much waste as possible at the very first step—the designing and manufacturing stage.

Products can be designed in ways that reduce waste. A lot of packaging is "instant garbage." Often there is too much of it and sometimes no packaging is needed at all. Only rarely does a company deliberately design a product or package for easy recycling or to reduce waste.

For many years, six-packs of beer were held together with cardboard cartons. Then some companies switched to a plastic harness that held six cans together at the top. This was a backward step. The plastic does not break down nearly as fast as cardboard, and the harnesses cause the death of gulls, ducks, and other birds which become tangled in them. The invention of the "pull tab" or "flip top" opener on beer and soft drink cans is another example of design *without* the environment in mind. These sharp-edged objects will litter the landscape for centuries.

The "Press Tab" opening remains attached to the can. It may replace the use of sharp-edged "pull tabs" which now litter North America.

In the early 1970s, the Adolph Coors Brewing Company of Colorado began testing some new ways to package beer and to open cans. The "Stik Pack" is six cans held together with glue. And the "Press Tab" folds into a can and stays attached to it. If these ideas are successful and replace "pull tabs" and the usual six-pack packaging, they will represent an extraordinary example of how thoughtful design can reduce solid wastes and litter.

More often, a company or industry changes a product in a way that makes it a burden on the environment. In the early 1970s, soft drink companies began enclosing large bottles in a sheath of Styrofoam plastic. The plastic was designed to reduce breakage in shipping and handling. But it has to be removed before bottles can be used as cullet, so the new packaging hampers recycling.

Some environmentalists suggest, "If returnable bottles are a good idea, why not make all glass containers returnable?" Food and drink companies often try to make their products noticeable by having a bottle or jar that is different from others. You can see a hundred different shapes and sizes of glass containers in a supermarket or liquor store.

If all glass containers came in a few standard shapes and sizes, they could be used again and again as returnable bottles are. The food and drink companies could identify and advertise the contents on the labels, as they do now. Of course this change would be opposed by store managers (who would have to handle and store the returnable containers) and by glass manufacturers (who would make fewer containers). However, most of the best ideas for reducing solid wastes and damage to the environ-

106

ment would affect the practices of the makers and sellers of products. Which is more important?

Solid wastes could be reduced if products were designed and built to last longer. Automobiles last about seven years; they could be built to last twice as long. And cars could also be designed so that their parts were more easily recycled. The zinc in cars could be replaced with steel; most of the copper could be replaced with steel or aluminum. The goal of redesigning cars (and thousands of other things) would be to have a more durable product made of fewer different kinds of materials which could be more easily separated.

Changes like these will not be made voluntarily by industries. Only some kind of federal program of rewards and penalties will cause widespread design for recycling.

Finally, the solid waste crisis will not be solved until people change their attitudes. Many people still act as though the environment were a free dump and resources were unlimited. But trash is our only growing resource. Other resources, especially fossil fuels and metals, are being consumed or mined at a rapid rate. The metals are still on earth, of course, but great amounts are disappearing into landfills, to the bottom of the ocean, and to other out-of-the-way places.

No nation can go on squandering resources like this. The people of one state—New Jersey—are expected to discard about 425 million tons of solid wastes between the years

Many brands of food have differently shaped containers.
They could be packed in sturdy returnable jars
of a few standard sizes.

1970 and 2000. The resources in this waste will be worth an estimated $6.4 billion.

No nation can afford to bury and burn these resources, or to go on damaging the environment by using new materials when used materials are available. Consider these savings in the steel industry, estimated by the Environmental Protection Agency: Making steel from scrap instead of ore requires 74 percent less energy and uses 40 percent less water. Using scrap steel instead of ore also reduces air pollution 86 percent, water pollution 76 percent, and mining waste 97 percent.

Recycling resources will have to become a way of life in the United States and other rich nations. There will have to be basic changes in government policies and laws, in industry practices, and in people's attitudes. The changes will not be easy, but landfill space, resources, and time are running out. The problem of the "Third Pollution" must get the attention it deserves.

what you can do

Solid waste problems will never be solved by the voluntary actions of individual citizens. Real solutions will come only from far-reaching changes in government and industry. And the solid waste mess will probably become more of a crisis before these changes are made.

Nevertheless, individuals can help ease solid waste problems and speed the day of real solutions. Here are some things you can do to help:

Avoid products that are overpackaged, such as cereals in single-serving boxes and fruit juices in single-serving cans. You pay more for the extra packaging. Buy food, laundry soap, and other products in the biggest containers available. A lot of packaging is instant garbage; avoid it wherever possible. When you buy only a few easy-to-carry items, say, "I don't need a bag," to store clerks.

Recycle as much material as you can, without doing the environment much harm in the process. In some areas, it is possible to recycle glass, newspapers, magazines, aluminum, and steel cans. Some paper companies also accept cartons such as the containers used for cereal, ice cream, and dry pet foods. (Cartons take up a lot of space; when you flatten them and save them for recycling, you will notice that the volume of trash you throw away is greatly reduced.)

Avoid using excess energy and adding to pollution in your efforts to recycle resources. Combine a trip to the recycling center with other errands. Team up with other families to bring materials to a recycling center in one big load, rather than several small ones. And if the nearest recycling center is many miles away, consider the idea that the environment may be better off if you do not try to save and recycle materials.

Join with others to help bring about real change in solid waste problems. There may be several groups in your community that are concerned about solid waste and other environmental problems. By combining forces, these groups may be able to change wasteful practices in schools, businesses, and government. For example, schools buy and use lots of paper. Do the schools in your community insist that paper they buy contain a high percentage of recycled fibers? Why not? The same question can be asked of banks, other businesses, and the government of your community. So far, the main obstacle to greater recycling of paper has been a lack of markets; this will change when enough customers insist on using recycled fibers.

Some community officials are interested in greater recycling efforts but hesitate because most citizens seem to care only that their trash is taken away at low cost. You can help educate people about the need for change from our wasteful ways. A number of cities ask their citizens to separate newspapers from trash, and then collect the

110

News about volunteer recycling efforts has helped many people realize the value of the things they throw away.

papers for sale and recycling. Other cities have purchased equipment which is used to recover steel cans from trash. You may be able to help your community adopt these important steps toward recovering resources and saving landfill space.

Industries spend millions of dollars to make their views of solid waste problems known to elected officials in state and federal governments. It is up to citizen groups and individuals to inform officials of their opinions. You can help by writing letters to state legislators and to senators and congressmen in Washington. Urge others to do the same. The combined efforts of many people are needed to convince government leaders to take actions that are really effective in solving solid waste problems.

further reading

Books and magazines marked with an asterisk (*) are fairly simple; the others are more difficult. For more up-to-date articles about recycling problems and progress, see recent issues of the magazine Environment, published by the Scientists' Institute for Public Information, 438 N. Skinker Boulevard, St. Louis, Missouri 63130.

*CANNON, JAMES, "Steel: The Recyclable Material." *Environment*, November 1973, pp. 11–20. Describes obstacles to greater recycling of iron and steel, especially obstacles within the steel industry itself.

CRUSBERG, THEODORE, *et al.*, *Solid Waste Management*. Worcester, Mass.: Worcester Polytechnic Institute, 1973. A 366-page report of a conference on solid wastes held in January 1973.

*DICKSON, EDWARD M., "Taking It Apart." *Environment*, July–August 1972, pp. 36–41. Using automobiles as an example, this article stresses the idea that products should be designed for recycling.

*GRINSTEAD, ROBERT R., "Bottlenecks." *Environment*, April 1972, pp. 2–13. Assesses the resources (such as metals, glass, paper) in trash, and some of the recycling difficulties they represent.

*——, "Machinery for Trash Mining." *Environment*, May 1972, pp. 34–42. Describes resource recovery systems and the main obstacles in the way of their widespread use.

*HANNON, BRUCE M., "Bottles, Cans, Energy." *Environment*, March 1972, pp. 11–21. Traces the development of throwaway containers and compares energy needed for their use with that needed for returnable containers.

*KASPER, WILLIAM C., "Power from Trash." *Environment*, March 1974, pp. 34–38. A look at efforts to use solid wastes as fuel for generating electricity.

*MCCAULL, JULIAN, "Back to Glass." *Environment*, January–February 1974, pp. 6–11. A progress report on the laws favoring returnable beverage containers in Oregon and Vermont.

*MARSHALL, JAMES, *Going to Waste: Where Will All the Garbage Go?* New York: Coward, McCann & Geoghegan, Inc., 1972. A basic introduction to the problem of solid wastes, and some possible solutions.

*NATIONAL ASSOCIATION OF RECYCLING INDUSTRIES, *Recycling Resources*, 1973. An informative 24-page booklit with emphasis on the need to develop markets for recyclable materials. Available from NARI, 330 Madison Avenue, New York, N.Y. 10017.

NEW JERSEY COUNTY AND MUNICIPAL GOVERNMENT STUDY COMMISSION SEVENTH REPORT. *Solid Waste: A Coordinated Approach.* September 1972. A 64-page report on solid waste problems in New Jersey, with recommendations for their solution.

*SOUCIE, GARY, "How You Gonna Keep It Down on the Farm?" *Audubon*, September 1972, pp. 113–115. "It" is agricultural wastes, and this article reports on the problems and opportunities represented by this huge but little-known part of solid wastes.

*——, "Solid Waste: The New Apocalypse." *Audubon*, January 1973, pp. 115–130. A report on solid wastes which gives special attention to political, social, and economic factors in this problem.

*——, "Tailings and Other Failings: A Story of Mining and Mineral Wastes," *Audubon,* May 1973, pp. 106–109. Describes the huge amounts of solid wastes produced by mineral and fossil fuel industries, and the problems they cause.

*UNITED STATES ENVIRONMENTAL PROTECTION AGENCY REPORT. *Solid Waste Management: Available Information Materials.* July 1973. A listing of over 300 booklets, studies, and other publications about solid wastes.

114

index

Asterisk (*) indicates photograph or drawing.

acid from plastics, 65–66
advertising, 19–20, 22, 23, 24, 26, 33–34, 55, 111
agricultural wastes, *13–14, 44
air pollution, 2, 4, 7, 10, 13, 42, 60, 65, 74, 79, 108
aluminum: amount recycled, 34, 36, 100; industry, 96; in solid wastes, 15, 70, 82, *101, 107; recycling of, 83, *84–*85, 86, 109; separation of, 46, 48, 79
American Paper Institute, 56
attitudes of people toward recycling and solid wastes, 4, 7, 20, 30, 69, 90, 103, 107, 108, 110
automobiles, 17, 69–79, 88, 107

bauxite, 83
Black Clawson Company, 46–50, 103
bottles, 2, 12, 17, 18, 20, 22–23, 24–25, 32, 34, 87, 88, 105
boxes, 18, 55, *56
brass, 36, 48, 74
Briarcliff Manor, New York, recycling, 31–33
bronze, 48
bubble packs, *18, 19

cans, 2, 12, 17, 18, 22, 24, 25, 32, 34, 44–45, 80, 82, 83, 88, 109, 111
Carbecue, 79
carbon black, 79
cardboard, 19, 53, 104
cartons, 18, 56, 104, 109–110

clay in paper, 55, 60–61
compost, *38, *39–41
Connecticut's recycling plans, 100
container industry, 19–20, 23, 26, 29, 33–34, 96
copper, 15, 36, 48, 74, 77, 79, 80, 82, 107
cullet, 86–87, 105

design of products for recycling, 103–107
dumps: 1, 3, 4, 7, 15, 37, 53, 56, 66, 79, 83, 86, 100; *see also* landfills

employment, 29–30
energy: and aluminum making, 83; and recycling paper, 54; and steel making, 108; and throwaway containers, 26, 29; from trash, 11, 41–44, 63–65, 100

fabrics, 36, 80, *88–*89, 90
feedlots, *13, 14
fertilizers, 14, 40, 41
Franklin, Ohio, resource recovery plant, 46–50, *47, *48–*49, 103
freight rates, 59, 93–94
fuels, *see* energy; natural gas; oil

garbage, 1, 4, 5, 23, 39, 54, 103, 109
Garden State Paper Company, 56, 59
glasphalt, *86, 87
glass, 7, 10, 15, *28, *35, 36, 39, 41, 46, 48, 70, 86, 100, 105, 109

Glass Containers Manufacturers Institute, 34
glass manufacturers, 22, 26, 29, 31, 96, 105
gold, 15, 36

Hackensack Meadowlands Development Commission, 9–10, 38–39
Hannon, Dr. Bruce M., 26, 29
hidden costs in products, 99–100, 109
Hydrapulper, 46

incinerators, 7, 9–10, 41, 42, 44, 45, 49, 53, 65, 74, 79, 80
India, wastes produced in, 17
ink in paper, 56, 59, 60, 63
iron, *see* steel

jars: 18, 87, 105; *see also* bottles; glass

Keep America Beautiful, Inc., 23–24
kitchen middens, 3

landfills, *2–*3, 4, *5–12, *6, *8, *11, *12, 15, 20, 32, 37, 38, 39, 41, 54, 56, 65, 66, 83, 100, 107, 111
laws: affecting recycling, 25–26, 70, 89–90, 93–94, 97–100, 107, 108, 111; against pollution, 7, 60, 74
lead, 36, 70, 74, 79, 82
Letts, Christopher, 33
Lindsay, John V., 94
Liquid Cyclone, 48
litter: 12, 18, 20, 23, *24, 26, 29, 69, 88, 104–105; studies of, 24–26
Los Angeles Times, 59

magazines, recycling of, 32, 55, 109
magnets for separating wastes, 45–46, 48, 74, *75, 80, *81
markets for recycled materials, 31, 40, 41, 50–51, 62, 76, 77, 80, 103, 110

metals: 7, 10, 18, 37, 39, 41, 44, 46, 70, 80, 107; *see also* specific metals
mining wastes, 13, 14–15, 108
mountains of trash, 5, *10, 11–12

National Association of Recycling Industries, 94
New Jersey, 9–10, 38, 100, 107
newspapers, 2, 32, 38, 39, 55, *57, 59, 60, 63, 91, 109, *111
newsprint, 56, 59

oil, 42, 44, 63, 79, 100
oil spill cleanup, 63
Oregon "bottle" law, 25
Owen, Dr. Edwin L., 83

packaging, 18–19, 30, 91, *98, 99, 100, 103, 109
paper: 2, 4, 5, 12, 15, 17, 18, 24, 36, 46, 49, 50, 51, 66, 110; sources of, 53, 89; uses of, 53, 63, 103; *see also* magazines; newspapers; newsprint
plastics, 2, 17, 18, 19, 25, 48, *64, 65–*67, 70, 83, 91, 93, 99, 104, 105
pulpwood, *58, *60–*61, 89
pyrolysis, 44, *45, 79

reclamation plants, *see* resource recovery plants
recycling: 12, 15, 26, 41, 44, 109–111; centers for, 26, 31–34, 37, 39, 50; obstacles to, 40–41, 66, 80, 83, 90, 96, 107, 110; *see also* materials such as glass, paper, steel
residues of incinerators, 7, 9, 44–45, 80
Resource Recovery Act, 97
resource recovery plants, 10, 45–51, *48–*49, *96, 97, 99, 100, 102–103
returnable bottles, 20–23, 25–30, 105
roofing felt, 48, 51, 56, 103
rubber, 48, 55, 79, 80, 89

116

sand, made from glass, 87–88
sanitary landfill, *see* landfill
Scharf, Jerome, 94
scrap industry, 36–37, 76, 77
scrap metal, 31, 36, 69, 70, 76, 77
  82, 108
secondary materials, *see* scrap industry; scrap metal; textiles
silver, 15, 36
solid wastes: amounts of, 1, 4, 9,
  12–13, 14, 17, 19, 53, 65, 79,
  88, 107, 108; as source of
  energy, 11, 41–44, 63–65, 100;
  collection of, 1, 9, 32, 100; de-
  fined, 1; disposal costs of, 4, 9,
  19, 20, 23, 32; kinds of, 1–2,
  13–14; separation of, 38–39, 41,
  80; *see also* recycling; specific
  materials such as aluminum,
  paper, tires
steel, 15, 22, 45, 46, 48, 70, 74, 76,
  77, 79, 80, 82, 83, 100, 107,
  108, 109, 111
steel industry, 22, 26, 29, 76, 82,
  96, 108
strip-mined land, *40, 41

tax benefits, laws, rates, 93–94, 96,
  99, 100
textiles, 48, 88–90
Third Pollution, 1, 2, 30, 108

throwaway containers: 19–30; *see
  also* bottles; cans
tin, in cans, 82
tires, 2, 17, *78, 79–80
trash, *see* solid wastes

Union Electric Power Company,
  St. Louis, 42
United States Army Laboratories,
  63
United States Bureau of Mines, 44,
  45, 70, 74, 77, 79, 97
United States Environmental Protection Agency, 34, 94, 97, 103,
  108
upholstery, 70, 89

Vermont "bottle" law, 26
Virginia Beach, site of Mt. Trashmore, 11–12

wallboard, 55, 56
water pollution, 4, 12, 13, 14, 15,
  30, 33, 60, 108
"white goods," *76–*77
Williams, Thomas F., 34
wood fibers (in paper), 53, 54–55,
  59, 61, 62, 63, 65
Wool Labeling Act, 89–90, 94

zinc, 70, 107

ALSO BY LAURENCE PRINGLE